PEDRO'S WHALE

by

Paula Kluth, Ph.D.
Independent Education Consultant and Scholar
Oak Park, Illinois

Patrick Schwarz, Ph.D.
Chief Executive Officer, Creative Culture Consulting, LLC
Professor
Department of Diversity in Learning & Teaching
National-Louis University
Chicago, Illinois

Illustrated by

Justin Canha
Freelance Illustrator and Artist
Montclair, New Jersey

·P·A·U·L·H·
BROOKES
PUBLISHING C°®

Baltimore • London • Sydney

Paul H. Brookes Publishing Co.
Post Office Box 10624
Baltimore, Maryland 21285-0624
USA

www.brookespublishing.com

"Paul H. Brookes Publishing Co." is a registered trademark of
Paul H. Brookes Publishing Co., Inc.

Typeset by Paul H. Brookes Publishing Co.
Manufactured in China by JADE PRODUCTIONS.

The individuals described in this book are composites of real people whose situations have been masked and are based on the author's experiences. Names and identifying details have been changed to protect confidentiality.

Library of Congress Cataloging-in-Publication Data
Kluth, Paula.
 Pedro's whale / by Paula Kluth, Patrick Schwarz ; illustrated by Justin Canha.
     p.   cm.
 ISBN-13: 978-1-59857-160-8 (pbk.)
 ISBN-10: 1-59857-160-5 (pbk.)
 1. Students with disabilities—Education (Elementary)—Juvenile literature. 2. Autism in children—Juvenile literature. 3. Whales—Juvenile literature. I. Schwarz, Patrick. II. Canha, Justin, ill. III. Title.
 LC4069.3.K58 2010
 618.92'89—dc22   2010019414

British Library Cataloguing in Publication data are available from the British Library.

2014   2013   2012   2011   2010

10   9   8   7   6   5   4   3   2   1

To every child and young adult who has a fascination that is
not always shared by others, including (but not limited to) whales,
steam engines, windshield wipers, weather, rubber bands, root
beer bottles, belt buckles, garage doors, American Idol, sharks,
license plates, pencil stubs, pre-1960s animation, poodles, world
leaders, record players, the Battles of Lexington and Concord,
vacuum cleaners, Madagascar, tractors, bus schedules, lighthouses,
robins, picket fences, Bing Crosby, and soup labels.

Preface

The publication of *"Just Give Him the Whale!"* prompted many readers to ask us about Pedro, the little boy who inspired our book title. Other readers wanted to know how to teach the notion of honoring fascinations to children. Educators wondered how to explain the practices we espoused to their students, and parents sought ways to talk to siblings about building on strengths in the home. All of these individuals inspired us to write **Pedro's Whale.**

This book is based on actual events that happened at a public school in Chicago. The story was brought to us by the school principal, a woman with a very optimistic view of learners and their potential. Pedro, the "star" of the story, is a young man who, although we do not allude to it in this book, is on the autism spectrum. We do not label him in the story because we believe the following message of **Pedro's Whale** is relevant for all learners:

> *Every child has fascinations, areas of expertise, and passions he or she brings to the school. As teachers, our job is to honor them! We need to exploit the "loves" of our learners, not extinguish them.*

More than anything in the world,
Pedro loved whales.

He loved BIG whales. He loved **grey** whales.
He loved *small* whales. He loved **blue** whales.

But most of all, he loved *his* whale.
It made him so happy.

Pedro could not wait for the first day of school.
He wanted to make pictures, sing songs,
and show everyone his whale.

He was very excited as he hung up his backpack.
And he was *very* excited as he took his whale
out to show his new friends.

But when his teacher, Ms. Tamayo,
saw his beautiful, shiny, fits-perfectly-in-a-pocket
whale, she smiled, held out her hand, and said,
"Sorry, Pedro, no toys during class."

Pedro gave Ms. Tamayo the whale.

Soon he felt a tear in his eye and then another.

Pedro cried harder and harder
and ducked under a table to hide.

Just then Pedro's principal, Ms. Gomez, came to the door and saw Pedro crying and crouching under the table.

Ms. Gomez asked Ms. Tamayo, "What's wrong with Pedro?"

Ms. Tamayo whispered, "Pedro brought a toy to school, and students are not allowed to play with toys during class."

Ms. Gomez said, "Pedro is new to our school, and he may need a little extra comfort and support. What is it that you want Pedro to do?"

Ms. Tamayo replied, "I want him to follow directions, sit with his classmates, and do his work."

Ms. Gomez smiled and explained, "New things are scary for Pedro. His whale helps him feel safe and do his best work. If you want Pedro to do his best work, you just need to *give him his whale!*"

Ms. Tamayo walked over to Pedro holding the whale. Slowly, he came out from under the table. She handed the toy back to him and said, "Ms. Gomez told me your whale helps you learn. Is that right?"

Pedro nodded and sniffled.

"Then let's see how the whale can help us all!"

After that, Pedro got to keep the whale at calendar time.
It helped him learn the days of the week and months of the year.

He got to keep it at storytime.
It helped him travel to faraway places.

Of course, he got to keep it during science.
It helped him learn about sinking and floating!

He even got to keep it at recess.
It helped him make new friends.

Even Ms. Tamayo used the whale
now and then.

Best of all...Pedro's classmates brought him
pictures of whales to use for his cubby,
and...

they even asked to go to the aquarium
to see the new baby whale for their field trip.

Pedro was very happy.
He loved kindergarten.

He loved his new teacher, his principal,
his new friends, and, of course...

his whale!

How to Use This Book

Pedro's Whale is a story of a child who not only needs his whale but who can be taught, comforted, and motivated when his special interest is brought into curriculum, instruction, and the classroom in general. Teachers who want to discuss with their class the special interests and needs of all students—or those who want to explain individual differences (e.g., autism) or curricular adaptations to the class—might use *Pedro's Whale* to do so. Activities that may be used with the story include the following:

- Talk about it. What collections do students have? What hobbies? What fascinations? Do any of the students in the group have the same fascinations? Do any of the students in the group have particularly unique fascinations? Do some students need to access their "favorites" more than others? How should students support classmates with a significant need to talk about, spend time with, or explore certain interests?

- Brainstorm as a group. Choose a student in the class who has a special interest. Let the class brainstorm 20, 30, or 50 ways to use that fascination to calm, comfort, teach, or amuse their classmate.

- Show and tell. Have students take turns bringing in items that have special meaning in their lives. Or, have students interview one another about their interests, fascinations, and areas of expertise.

- **Advertise.** Have students create help wanted and classified advertisements related to their needs and their fascinations. Help wanted ads communicate areas in which each student needs help (e.g., "I need help with reading"). Classified ads help students boast about something they can offer others (e.g., "I can teach about battleships"). Such ads can be posted on a classroom bulletin board and updated regularly. Students can then be encouraged to "answer" ads from peers—thereby providing opportunities for every learner to give and get help throughout the year.

- **Let them plan their own supports.** Give older students a copy of ***"Just Give Him the Whale!"*** (the companion text for this book) to browse, and then ask them to identify ideas they find appealing. This may prompt a helpful discussion or even help a team craft formal adaptations or individualized education program (IEP) goals.

Parents can also use this book to discuss special interests with their children and to explore ways to use, support, or even limit "favorites" in appropriate and respectful ways. Activities that might be used in the home include the following:

- **Learn to read and read to teach.** Some children may want to learn to read ***Pedro's Whale*** (independently or with the use of augmentative and alternative communication) and then share it with their therapists, friends, or family members as a way to communicate the need for others to respect their fascinations.

- **Start a conversation.** Use Pedro's situation as a springboard for discussing fears, challenges, and anxieties. Children who struggle to manage the time they spend on their special interest or those who feel oppressed by others because of their "loves" may find it easier to discuss Pedro's situation rather than their own. Parents may gain insight into their child's needs, beliefs, and difficulties by simply listening to how they understand and respond to Pedro's dilemma.

- **Teach advocacy.** *Pedro's Whale* can be used to teach students about their individual needs. It can even be used as a tool to teach self-advocacy. For example, parents may help their children see "obsessions" as fascinations.

- **Prepare for an IEP meeting.** Read the book a few times to prepare the child to share his or her own special interests with teachers at an educational planning meeting.

- **Inspire authorship.** Children can create their own picture books to tell their stories about their fascinations and to develop ideas for their own supports.

If you have other ideas about how this story can be used in the classroom or in the home, send them to us at paula.kluth@gmail.com or pschwarz@nl.edu.

About the Authors

PAULA KLUTH, PH.D., is one of today's most popular and respected experts on autism and inclusive education. Through her work as an independent consultant and presenter, Dr. Kluth helps professionals and families create responsive, engaging schooling experiences for students with disabilities and their peers, too. An internationally respected scholar and author, Dr. Kluth has written or cowritten several books for Paul H. Brookes Publishing Co., including *"A Land We Can Share": Teaching Literacy to Students with Autism* (2008); *"Just Give Him the Whale!": 20 Ways to Use Fascinations, Areas of Expertise, and Strengths to Support Students with Autism* (2008); and *"You're Going to Love This Kid!": Teaching Students with Autism in the Inclusive Classroom, Second Edition* (2010). Her popular web site can be found at http://www.paulakluth.com. Dr. Kluth is also on Facebook.

PATRICK SCHWARZ, PH.D., is Professor of Diversity in Learning & Teaching for National-Louis University, Chicago. A dynamic author and motivational speaker, Dr. Schwarz is also Chief Executive Officer of Creative Culture Consulting, LLC. His books *From Disability to Possibility: The Power of Inclusive Classrooms* (Heinemann, 2006); *You're Welcome: 30 Innovative Ideas for the Inclusive Classroom* (Heinemann, 2007); and *"Just Give Him the Whale!": 20 Ways to Use Fascinations, Areas of Expertise, and Strengths to Support Students with Autism* (2008) have inspired teachers nationwide to reconceptualize inclusion in ways that help all children. Dr. Schwarz's professional focus is furthering education and services that promote the status of individuals with a range of support needs. He works to facilitate successful engagement in various environments, allowing people to make contributions and develop experiences that are meaningful to them.

About the Illustrator

 **JUSTIN CANHA** is an accomplished artist who also happens to have autism. His childhood passion for drawing animals and cartoon characters revealed an innate talent that attracted the attention of the mainstream art community when Justin was 14 years old. Justin explores a wide range of subjects that showcase his clever sense of humor and unusual sensitivity to human and animal relationships. Featuring unique characters he has created, Justin's computer animations are full of action-packed stories, while his paintings celebrate still life and portraiture. Justin's drawings and illustrations demonstrate the intensity and perspective of the autistic mind and serve as a powerful form of communication.

Justin first appeared on the New York art scene in the well-received Autism/Aspergers Art Exhibit in January of 2005. Since then, Justin's career has been steadily gaining momentum. He received an Honorable Mention at the Studio Montclair Taboo Exhibition, and portions of his animations were recently incorporated into a hip-hop music video. Justin's work has been shown at the Beacon Firehouse Gallery, Montclair State University, Montclair's Luna Stage Theatre, The Cooper Union, and the Rhode Island Convention Center. Justin had solo exhibits at the Montclair Public Library, at Pace University, and most recently at the JCC in Manhattan and at Bloomfield College. Justin's artwork has been featured at the Ricco/Maresca booth at the Outsiders Fair in New York City; in *Sidecars,* a short documentary by Ben Stamper; and in *Autism: Communicating in a Different Way,* a documentary by Gary Keys. It also was shown in the August 2006 issue of *O, The Oprah Magazine.* In April 2009, his art work was shown at Art Chicago, the world-renowned international contemporary and modern art fair. Most recently, Justin's artwork was exhibited at the Morris Museum in *Timeless: The Art of Drawing* and at Adelphi University. In October 2009, Justin received an award for his artistic achievement at the Louder Than Words autism benefit held at Montclair State University.

In addition to illustrating *Pedro's Whale,* Justin's illustration commissions include the cover of *"Just Give Him the Whale!"* as well as a new line of math books for young children on the spectrum called *IBET (Integrated Behavioral Experiential Teaching).*

Justin is presently taking college-level courses in cartooning and animation at Bloomfield College, Montclair State University, and Pace University and working in the community in Montclair. For more information on Justin and to see more of his artwork and his animations, visit his web site: http://www.justinart.com.